W9-BHG-616

Urban Planner

Helen Mason

Gareth Stevens
PUBLISHING

Please visit our website, **www.garethstevens.com**. For a free color catalog of all our high-quality books, call toll free 1-800-542-2595 or fax 1-877-542-2596.

Library of Congress Cataloging-in-Publication Data

Mason, Helen.
Urban planner / by Helen Mason.
p. cm. — (Creative careers)
Includes index.
ISBN 978-1-4824-1353-3 (pbk.)
ISBN 978-1-4824-0933-8 (6-pack)
ISBN 978-1-4824-1451-6 (library binding)
1. City planning — Vocational guidance — United States. 2. City planning — Vocational guidance. 3. City planning — Vocational guidance — Juvenile literature. I. Mason, Helen, 1950-. II. Title.
HT167.M37 2015
307.1—d23

First Edition

Published in 2015 by
Gareth Stevens Publishing
111 East 14th Street, Suite 349
New York, NY 10003

Developed and produced for Gareth Stevens Publishing by BlueApple*Works* Inc.
Editor: Marcia Abramson
Art Director: Melissa McClellan
Designer: Joshua Avramson

Photo Credits: Dreamstime: © Randy Mckown, p. 4 bottom, p. 8 bottom, p. 41 bottom; © Maomaotou p. 5; © Jun He p. 6; © Colleen Coombe p. 7; © Melissa King p. 9 top; © Gabriel Eckert p. 9; © Tupungato p. 10 top; © Jerryb8 p. 10; © Aaron Kohr p. 11; © Photawa p. 12 top; © Jlindsay p. 12; © Timrobertsaerial p. 14 top; © Celso Diniz p. 14; © James Crawford p. 15; © Graham Prentice p. 16; © Bambi L. Dingman p. 18 top; © Ackphoto p. 23; © Mikhail Kusayev p. 27; © Mellie430 p. 28; © Carroteater p. 29 top; © Matt Antonino p. 29; © Michael Flippo p. 32 top; © Bigapplestock p. 38 top; © Photographer-london p. 38; © Dtguy p. 39; © Ulisse3 p. 42 top; © Tompenpark p. 43; © Monkey Business Images p. 44 top; © Mauricio Jordan De Souza Coelho p. 44; Shutterstock: © Richard Cavalleri cover top left; © Ant Clausen cover top right; © zhu difeng cover bottom left; © PHB.cz (Richard Semik) cover bottom right; © XiXinXing title p.; © Josef Hanus toc p. background; © Chardchanin toc p. ; © Tatsianama p. 4 left; © Andrey Bayda p. 5 bottom; © Richard Laschon p. 8 top; © TFoxFoto p. 13; © Lissandra Melo p. 16 top; © Kushal Bose p. 17; © spirit of america p. 18; © Mike Tan p. 19 left; © Monkey Business Images p. 19 right; © Zack Frank p. 20; © Jacek Chabraszewski p. 22 top; © Ocean Image Photography p. 22; © Halfpoint p. 24; © Albert Pego p. 25; © chungking p. 26; © Orhan Cam p. 28 top; © Richard Cavalleri p. 30 top; © Steven Wright p. 30; © nulinukas p. 31; © bikeriderlondon p. 32; © Pete Spiro p. 33 left; © Dragon Images p. 33 right, 37; © Andresr p. 34 top; © Fleming Photography p. 34; © Forster Forest p. 35; © jl661227 p. 37 top; Golden Pixels LLC p. 45 top; Courtesy of NORA: The New Orleans Redevelopment Authority. p. 20 top, p. 21; Public Domain/Phil Stanziola p. 40 top; © Rebecca Vaughan p. 40 middle; Graphic by Green Map System Graphic by Green Map System p. 40 bottom; Public Domain p. 41 right, p. 42; Public Domain/Al Ravenna p. 43 top

Manufactured in the United States of America

CPSIA compliance information: Batch #CS15GS. For further information contact Gareth Stevens, New York, New York at 1-800-542-2595.

Contents

What Is an Urban Planner?

Do you like people? Are you interested in cities? Do you enjoy dreaming about the future? If you answered yes to any of these questions, you might enjoy being an urban planner.

Towns and cities are urban areas. Urban planners design ways that they might look in the future.

Urban planners start with research. They must consider the following:

○ Where is the city?
○ What is the city like now?
○ How many people are there?
○ Where do they live?
○ What work do they do?
○ How do they move around the city?
○ How do they move the things they make and sell?
○ What type of recreation do they enjoy? Where?

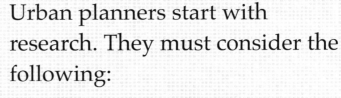

▲ *Urban planners create master plans for cities.*

4

The Master Plan

Urban planners listen to people. They try to learn how people feel about their city.

Urban planners decide what is and is not working well. Then, they make up a master plan for the city. This communicates how the city will look in the future. It describes what types of roads, buildings, and parks it will have. The plan may also make suggestions for creating jobs and protecting the environment. The government officials use that plan in making their decisions.

▼ Master plans consider the plants and animals in the area. They plan for parks and other green spaces.

▼ The San Francisco Planning Department plays a central role in guiding the growth and development of its city.

Types of Urban Planners

Urban planners help cities, towns, and even larger regions make decisions about their long-term futures. If the city is well-planned, people will always want to live and work there.

City Jobs

All cities have a plan. Urban planners help them look 20 to 30 years ahead. A city plan suggests how the city should look by that time. A growing city needs a plan for new construction that also preserves the environment. An older city needs a plan to attract residents and keep neighborhoods in good shape.

▼ Downtown plans often outline what new office buildings must include. They also provide suggestions for handling **commuter** traffic as workers move in and out of the downtown area.

Regional Jobs

Some areas have cities and towns that are close together. These places often belong to a regional municipality. The municipality includes the cities and their **suburbs**. The member cities plan together and cooperate to develop plans for transportation and land use.

Private Jobs

Community groups work on neighborhood issues. Some may hire a planner to help them.

Some towns are too small to have their own planner, while others need someone with special expertise. These places hire planning consultants. Consultants are often planners, architects, and engineers. These people work together to help cities plan for the future.

▼ *A planner mapped out where to put the streets, sewers, water lines, and parks in this development.*

Land-Use Planners

Some planners specialize in how land is used. These planners gather the following information:

○ Where do most of the people live?
○ Where are the factories?
○ Where are the stores and malls?
○ What natural features are present?
○ What highways and railroads go through the area?

▲ *This map shows the planned land use for part of a city.*

Planning Policies

Land-use planners work closely with government officials. They may work for the city directly or as a consultant. If a large area is available for development, they come up with ideas and locations for subdivisions, parks, industrial areas, and other land uses. They help cities consider proposals from private developers. A land-use planner also may process applications for development permits and **zoning** changes.

Land-Use Decisions

Land-use planners develop a plan that shows how the land should be used. Most plans include a certain amount of green space. Green spaces include parks, cemeteries, and farms.

Plans also include residential areas. These are the houses and apartment buildings where people live. Industrial areas are set aside for factories.

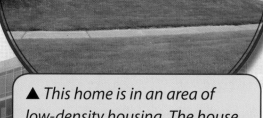

▼ These dwellings are in an area of medium-density housing. More people can live on the same amount of land than in the photo at right.

▲ This home is in an area of low-density housing. The house and its yard take up a lot of room.

9

Transportation Planners

Transportation involves moving people and the things they need. Transportation planners look at any problems related to transportation. For example, many people travel to work at the same time. This causes traffic jams. What if people started and ended their workday at different times? This might lower the number of cars during rush hour.

Highways, railway lines, and airports are expensive to build and maintain. Planners suggest where and when they will be needed.

▲ *Chicago has a good public transit system of buses, trains, and subways.*

▼ *Commuter trains and buses link suburban areas to cities so people can get to work.*

Road Networks

What is the best way for commuters to get to work? Some cities plan roads directly into those areas. Others have one-way streets. Drivers take one street to get into the city and another to get out. Many city plans encourage carpooling, or sharing a vehicle with others.

Public Transit

Public transit moves a lot of people fast. Commuter trains bring people into the city. City subways, buses, and streetcars get them where they are going. Public transit makes a city easier to live in. It's inexpensive and anyone can use it. When people walk more and drive less, they are healthier.

Subways carry one-third of commuters in the United States. Building subways is time-consuming and expensive. The route and plans for getting the money are part of the city plan.

◀ Cars and trucks use a lot of fossil fuels and cause pollution.

RIGHT LANES

Environmental Planners

Environmental planners try to develop ways to minimize the pollution cities cause. They also figure out ways to protect green spaces and wildlife.

Preserving Natural Resources

Natural resources include the air, water, and land. Some planners work to preserve these resources.

They study cities and calculate how much water is being used. They work with engineers to clean the water so that it can be reused. They also suggest how water can be **conserved**. Some make a list of local plants and animals. They research their needs and figure out how to keep them healthy.

▲ *Many city plans encourage the use of solar energy.*

▼ *New York City is working to reduce the type of pollution that causes global warming.*

Dealing with Climate Change

Burning fossil fuels such as coal, gas, and oil increases the amount of carbon dioxide in the Earth's atmosphere. Scientists say that this is causing an increase in the Earth's temperatures, a phenomenon known as global warming. As a result, sea levels are rising and weather patterns are changing. There are more big droughts and storms. Cities must be ready to respond to these changing conditions.

Some cities have developed plans to deal with global warming. These plans include the use of **alternative energy,** such as solar and wind. They also encourage the use of public transit and carpooling. In many areas, green building standards have been added to building codes.

▼ The plan for Portland, Oregon, increased the use of public transit.

Economic Development Planners

Economic development planners assess the good things about a city. They use these to create jobs. Their plans are revised every three to five years as businesses change.

Attracting Business

The planners talk to business owners. For example, they might approach a large chain store. They explain why the city is a good place to build a new store. If the

▲ *Many industrial parks are located just outside a city, where it is easy to get to them.*

store is interested, the city plan may be revised to allow this type of land use.

Some cities set aside land for factories. These areas are called **industrial parks**. The park is usually near major highways or railroads. Electricity and water lines, gas pipes, and sewers are already in place. Economic planners talk to factory owners about building new factories there.

▼ *City planners often place malls on or near highways.*

Creating Jobs

Economic development planners look for ways to create jobs. For example, a community college might be training people to create animated cartoons. The planner would contact movie and TV producers and encourage them to build a studio nearby. Some planners travel all over the world to convince businesses to locate in their area.

Another way to create jobs is through state and federal government programs. The government provides money for building or rebuilding businesses, especially in areas that are older or have suffered a natural disaster. Planners encourage and coordinate the government's assistance. By planning for population changes and studying employment trends, cities try to make sure that land is ready for future development.

▼ Craft markets such as the Saturday Market in Portland, Oregon, provide an economic outlet for artists and bring visitors to the area.

Urban Design Planners

Urban design planners also learn about **architecture** and landscaping. They look at a city's design and the appearance of its land.

City Design

A city's buildings, streets, and neighborhoods go together to make its design. Urban designers make sure that they look good and are useful. Well-designed streets are attractive. They have good sidewalks and allow traffic to move freely.

Urban design planners make sure that cities provide all essential services. Their plans include schools, hospitals, and police and fire protection. They also cover water treatment facilities, buried pipes, and power plants.

◀ Water treatment facilities and sewer lines may last 50 to 100 years. Planners decide where to place them, as well as how to maintain and replace them.

Planning Exercises

Urban design planners meet with the public and ask how they want the community to look in the future. These ideas may become part of their plans.

Special meetings called public hearings must be held before big changes can be made in an area. Anyone can attend and comment. Planners also use surveys to find out what the public wants.

▼ Austin, Texas, started its 2009 plan by developing and handing out a booklet that explained the process and how to get involved.

Housing Planners

Housing planners look at the way the city is now. They study the quality, age, and condition of city housing. They also look at who owns it.

Housing planners forecast how many people will need housing in the future and plan the number and type of homes that will be needed.

▲ Boulder, Colorado, limits the number of new houses that can be built each year. This reduces new demands for water, city services, and schools.

Affordable Housing

Many people cannot afford to buy or maintain large homes. Housing planners encourage people to build affordable housing, such as **duplexes** and row houses. People with limited income can better afford these homes.

▼ Row housing increases the number of people who can live on a piece of land.

Public and Community Housing

Housing planners also plan public and community housing. **Public housing** is owned by the government. People pay rent according to how much income they have.

People who cannot live on their own are often in community housing where a small number of people live together in a single home. The home is owned by the government. The government pays people to help the residents take care of themselves.

▼ Between 1946 and 1964, large numbers of children were born to American families. As they age, these baby boomers will need more retirement homes.

▶ Many people live in units such as this. The residents need services such as schools, hospitals, and fire stations.

Talking to an Urban Planner

Jeffrey Hébert, New Orleans

In 2005, Hurricane Katrina hit New Orleans, flooding 80 percent of the city. Jeffrey Hébert moved back to New Orleans to help rebuild it.

▲ *Jeffrey Hébert has an undergraduate degree in urban development and architecture. His master's degree is in city planning.*

How long have you worked as an urban planner?

I've been an urban planner for 12 years, in places such as New York and Philadelphia. In 2010, I became the Executive Director of the New Orleans Redevelopment Authority.

◀ *Hurricane Katrina destroyed homes, businesses, roads, and just about everything else in large areas of Louisiana. Katrina caused more than $108 billion in damage—the most for any hurricane in US history.*

Can you explain what you do?

Hurricane Katrina destroyed a lot of properties. We have to rehabilitate, rebuild, and replace structures.

My work starts with interviewing people to learn about their needs. Then I develop a plan to meet those needs. I help to raise funds. This includes getting money from the federal government, charitable organizations, and financial institutions. Once we have the money, I oversee implementing the plan. Then it's time to check that everything was done correctly and that people are happy.

Describe one project that you're particularly proud of.

We worked with the Make It Right Foundation to build high-quality, environmentally friendly homes in the Lower Ninth Ward. That's the area worst hit by the storm. Work on the homes has helped redevelop the community. There is a sense of everyone working together.

▶ A fun part of Hébert's job is to attend celebrations. This ribbon-cutting ceremony was for new housing.

The Work

Asking Questions

Urban planners meet with government officials and the public. They gather information by asking questions such as:

- What types of houses do people have?
- Where do they work?
- How do they travel?
- How is the land being used?

Analyzing Data

Urban planners study the answers. Then they ask themselves:

- How can we make this a better place?
- What will happen if we follow these ideas?
- What will happen if we do nothing?

▲ *The plan for Minneapolis, Minnesota, included 130 miles (209 km) of bike lanes.*

▼ *Planners think that Anaheim, California, will need 160,000 more acres by 2030. The city plan figures out where to place roads, sewers, and water pipes.*

Suggesting Ideas

Next, urban planners suggest changes. Their suggestions depend on the area.

In a city with empty factories, they might suggest replacing them with parks. Perhaps one of those could be a dog park. If a lot of people are out of work, they might develop ideas for bringing in new jobs.

Sometimes urban planners have a surprising vision for an area. They may suggest turning abandoned urban areas into large farms, or tearing down a freeway that is not used much anymore to make the land into a park.

▼ Ferry service is part of many city plans. The Staten Island Ferry in New York City carries more than 21 million passengers annually.

The Planning Process

A city plan starts with the city's vision of itself. If the city wants people to vacation there, then hotels and restaurants are important. If the city wants to attract a major industry, then roads, utilities, and housing are key needs.

Here is how a plan is developed.

Steps in Planning

1. Assess what you have.

   ○ Get information about the people. How many are there? What is their income?
   ○ Research land use, housing, transportation, natural resources, and public services.

2. Create goals.

   ○ What does the community want for the next 20 to 50 years?

▶ *Planners involve people in many ways. They host meetings and focus groups, plus conduct interviews and surveys.*

3. Decide what actions to take.

○ Develop actions that help meet each goal.

○ If the community wants more open space, the plan will need to provide ways to get this.

4. Decide how to implement, monitor, and update the plan.

○ Decide how to evaluate the results of each action.
○ Plan how to implement each one.
○ Consider how to keep an eye on progress.
○ Decide how and when to update the plan.

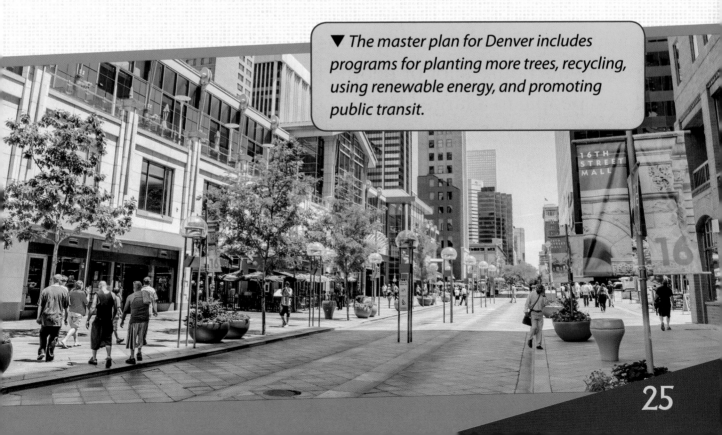

▼ The master plan for Denver includes programs for planting more trees, recycling, using renewable energy, and promoting public transit.

Challenges Today

Today's cities have three main problems. One is urban sprawl, which is when cities take over the land around them. The second is the amount of land it takes to handle all the natural resources a city uses. This is called an **ecological footprint**. The third is how to protect cities from disasters.

Urban Sprawl

When cities spill out into adjoining land, green space and farmland are taken away. Urban sprawl also leads to a car-dependent culture. The farther you live from where you work means less free time. More traffic also means more pollution. One way to counter this is to make city neighborhoods safe and attractive. Row housing and apartments house a lot of people in a small space, instead of few people in a large space.

▼ Urban sprawl can make it difficult for people to get from the suburbs to work in the city.

Ecological Footprint

Planners look for ways to protect natural resources. Bike lanes, for example, reduce car use. Planners also encourage green buildings. These use fewer fossil fuels, create less waste, and use less water.

Disaster Planning

Planners prepare for disasters such as earthquakes, oil spills, and terrorism. They identify threats and try to prevent them. For example, they may stop people from building in places where a river floods.

They also may plan evacuation routes and places for people to stay during a disaster.

◄ Urban planners can play a role in helping cities to be better prepared and resilient when it comes to natural disasters.

Modern Renewal

Many US cities have lost businesses and people. The cities need to change. This change is called **urban renewal**.

Build on What You Have

Planners look at what a city has or does well. They may create parks and walkways along any body of water. These projects create

▲ *Downtown areas are close to many services. Their presence attracts people who fix up older homes.*

jobs. The area may attract shops and cafés that encourage people to visit. These changes attract tourists. People open businesses to serve the tourists. That makes more jobs.

improve city ➡ attract new businesses ➡ create jobs ➡ attract new residents

▼*In Kansas City, Missouri, an old railway station was redesigned to house a museum, restaurants, shops, and a theater.*

Improve the Downtown

Many cities start with the downtown. Empty factories may become housing or fancy restaurants. This attracts people. They live there and work in nearby government buildings and businesses.

The presence of water makes a downtown even more attractive. Indianapolis designed a canal walk through its downtown. The walk connects to parks, hotels, apartments, offices, and schools. People can bike, walk, kayak, or even paddle boat. It's a great place to live and work.

▲ The Indy 500 attracts thousands to Indianapolis, Indiana. The annual car race has led to many local businesses related to cars and sports.

▼ Pittsburgh turned industrial land into Point State Park. People use the green space to relax and for concerts and festivals. They live and work nearby.

How Streets Are Changing

The way that streets are organized has changed over the years. No one planned streets for cars before they were invented! Today's urban planners try to think ahead and design for the future.

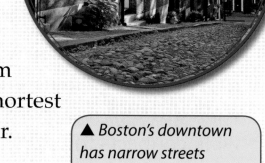

Organic Structure

Streets in early cities developed from the paths. The paths followed the shortest way to get from one place to another. This is called an organic structure.

▲ Boston's downtown has narrow streets paved with cobblestone.

Old Boston has this type of street pattern. This city developed on a peninsula. The streets moved inland from the harbor. Beacon Hill still has streets with many original row houses. The streets meet at odd angles, just as paths do.

▶ Manhattan's grid pattern is still visible. Streets run at right angles to avenues.

Grid Pattern

John Randel, Jr. laid out streets in what is now Manhattan in 1811. His plan used a grid pattern, with streets at right angles. The pattern is still visible today.

Modern Techniques

Today, many areas are built around automobiles. Highways and freeways provide fast transit, but they are noisy. Planners create noise barriers and keep neighborhood streets safe and quiet.

Planners use several methods to make streets safe for **pedestrians**. Some streets have speed bumps. Many subdivisions have through roads bordered by cul-de-sacs. Dead-end streets reduce the number of cars, making streets safer for pedestrians.

▼ *Speed bumps are used to slow traffic and discourage cars from using the street as a thoroughfare.*

Related Careers

Many careers use similar skills to those needed for urban planning. Developers plan new housing. Marketers help attract tourists. Demographers predict how the population will likely change.

▲ Historians help preserve buildings that have a special place in history.

Architects

Architects, like urban planners, envision how a city could be. They work with urban planners when developing large office buildings or condominiums to make sure their vision fits with the city plans. Architects draw up plans for buildings. Some design green buildings that use less energy to run. Architects may also design parks and other spaces the community uses for special celebrations.

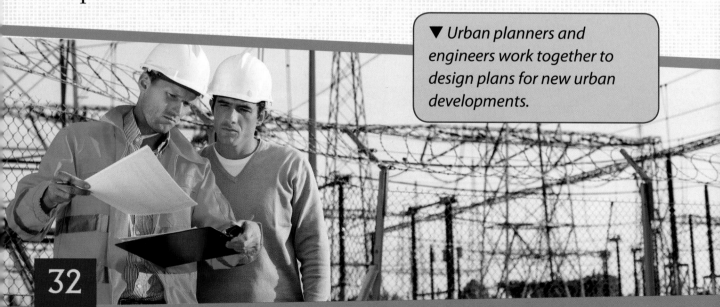

▼ Urban planners and engineers work together to design plans for new urban developments.

Engineers

Cities have a lot of structures. Engineers plan and evaluate building projects. Some design roads that are safe for cars and trucks. They also place stop signs and lights. Other engineers plan and build bridges and canals.

Environmental engineers study how cities affect the environment. They make suggestions on how to reduce environmental damage.

Historians and Lawyers

Historians study a city's history and provide ideas for preserving it. They might work in historic preservation for a municipal government or non-profit organizations. Lawyers help develop new laws that support the city's plans and projects.

◄ Bridges last a long time, but require people to maintain them. Engineers check their structure to ensure they are safe.

33

How to Become an Urban Planner

Interested in becoming an urban planner? You can start learning the skills now. Get to know your street, town, and region. What would make them better? Maybe families would like to have a community garden, a leash-free zone, or a skateboard park. Talk to your friends and neighbors. Being able to talk to people and find out their needs is an important skill for urban planners.

▲ *A leash-free zone, or dog park, is a great place for family fun.*

▼ *Community gardens benefit people and the environment.*

Community Garden

Research

Now that you have some ideas, check out what is actually being planned for your area. Find your city plan online, at the library, or at city hall. You will learn valuable research skills.

Mapping Skills

You'll need to read and even create maps as an urban planner. Join an orienteering club and have fun while learning about mapping. Orienteering is a timed race during which people follow clues and use a map and compass as they make their way across rough country.

▼ *Learn how to read maps well by orienteering. You will have fun and learn, too.*

Getting Experience

Now that you have some planning ideas, start taking part in community affairs. You can see how city planning is handled and how to get involved.

Attend Public Meetings

Find out what is happening in your community. Attend public meetings. Study the way planners handle the meeting. Get up and explain your ideas. Public speaking is an important skill. Practice by getting up and speaking at school and local meetings.

Become a Youth Representative

Many community groups are concerned about what is happening in your city and country. They want input from young people. Consider joining one or offer to be the youth representative. Attend meetings and learn how to influence government decisions. Listen to discussions and consider the issues. Some decisions will affect young people. Find out how people you know feel about the issue. Report back.

Become an Activist

Many schools have groups that work with the teachers and principal on school issues. Join one of these groups and learn how to make changes.

Play Planning Games

You can practice urban planning and have fun at the same time! There are many computer games in which players design and build a city. Their job is to keep people happy and spend government money wisely. Players place electricity and water lines. They handle waste management and decide on development zones. They may also deal with a disaster. This is good training for the real thing. There also are fun board games that feature urban planning, such as *Ticket to Ride*.

▲ *City building games allow users to create realistic looking 3D city models.*

▼ *Many community groups want input from young people. Offer to research young people's opinions. Then, present them to the group.*

Advanced Education

Urban planning is a growing field that requires advanced education.

Go to College

After high school, attend a college or university. Study what interests you.

Planners often study urban design. Some study English, art, or history. Others take classes in sociology (how society works), economics (how money works), or civics (how government works). Still others get degrees in public health, social work, nursing, or engineering.

▲ *You need to earn at least two degrees to be an urban planner. You may go to a different college for each one.*

▼ *A bachelor's degree comes first, then a master's in urban planning.*

Graduate School

To be an urban planner, you need a master's degree in urban planning. You will need good grades in college to be accepted to graduate school.

Internship

Become an urban planning **intern**. You will work with urban planners. Although your pay will be low, you will learn important skills and these will help you get a job after college.

Some people work as interns in another country. They learn how other countries solve problems and then use these ideas to help them solve problems at home.

▼ People in other countries have learned how to handle large numbers of people in a small space. This information will be useful for US planners.

Urban Difference Makers

Woman with a Vision

Jane Jacobs (1916–2006) encouraged planners to study neighborhoods and listen to people. She believed that cities need a variety of buildings, including ones for businesses and housing. Neighborhoods with both types are safer and healthier.

▲ Jane Jacobs was against building freeways. She encouraged mixed-use neighborhoods.

▲ Wendy Brawer is the founder and Director of Green Map Systems. People are encouraged to help create green maps of their communities.

Green Map Maker

In 1992, Wendy Brawer made the first green map. Green maps show where a city's natural resources are. They include recycling centers, historic sites, and toxic waste sites. The maps make people more aware of what they want to protect and what may cause problems.

Leaders in Rethinking

During the last 50 years, many communities have built gigantic malls and parking lots. Today, many of these are empty. Ellen Dunham-Jones and June Williamson encourage people to reuse these spaces. Parking lots can be turned into park land or developed to create business offices and housing. Malls can be redesigned as schools and housing.

Pedestrian Advocate

Michael Arth wants to lower automobile use. His plans show houses that face a walkway rather than a road. This encourages people to walk, cycle, or skate. Trees line the walkway, forming a park-like area. Automobile traffic is behind the houses.

▼ Ellen Dunham-Jones and June Williamson have new ideas for the suburbs.

▼ Born in 1953, Michael Arth designs communities that encourage walkers.

How Urban Planning Evolved

American urban planning began in the late 1800s. In California, cities developed laws about where laundries, pool halls, and livery stables could be built.

The first national conference on city planning was in Washington, DC, in 1909. At first, people worked on how cities looked. Gradually, planners began to study how to make cities more efficient. They also learned more about protecting the environment.

▲ The famed architect, Le Corbusier (1887–1965), designed the influential Unité d'Habitation, an apartment building in a park setting, with large open living spaces, shops, meeting rooms, and rooftop garden.

▼ The large and showy buildings at the 1893 Chicago World's Fair were America's original taste of urban planning.

Planning Cities

Edward Bassett (1863–1948) helped to plan New York City's subway. In 1916, he authored the United States' first laws that divided a city into zones for different purposes.

Lewis Mumford (1895–1990) suggested that how people relate to the places they live is important. This can make people healthy or sick. According to him, good planning considers the environment.

Frank Lloyd Wright (1867–1959) is often considered the greatest American architect of all time. He designed modern homes in planned communities.

▼ *Frank Lloyd Wright's ideas are used in many suburbs.*

You Can Be an Urban Planner

Do you still want to be an urban planner? Check out the following list. Which traits do you have? Which ones are you developing?

▲ *Some high school classes get involved in community planning. If your school has a program like this, take it.*

I am

☐ hardworking
☐ able to use a computer
☐ organized
☐ able to write clearly

I enjoy

☐ working with people
☐ studying how people live
☐ developing new ideas
☐ listening to different points of view

If you have or are developing these traits, you might make a great urban planner.

▼ *Volunteering will teach you a lot about your community. Check out www.idealist.org to find opportunities in your area.*

Set Your Goal

Decide what area of urban planning interests you. Research the needed training either online or by talking to a guidance counselor.

○ What high school subjects will help you prepare?

○ What schools offer the program you want?

○ What grades do you need?

Take Steps Now

Start today. Spend extra time on the subjects you need. These include geography and civics.

Join any school clubs that develop mapping, public speaking, or government skills.

Many states have a page program where teens live in a state capital and assist an elected official. Research your state's page program. Consider applying.

Try to get a summer job working with people. This could be as a camp counselor or tour guide.

▲ *Take part in a peer mediation program if your school has one. Urban planners often have to resolve conflicting views and seek compromises.*

Glossary

alternative energy sources of power that do not use fossil fuels, such as solar and wind

architecture a method or style of making buildings

commuter a person who travels from one place to another, especially from home to work and back

conserve to use carefully, not wastefully, or to keep in safe condition

cul-de-sac a street that is closed at one end

duplex two separate homes that share one common wall

ecological footprint a measure of the impact humans have on the environment, including land use and pollution

greenbelt a strip of landscaped areas, parks, or farms that encircles a community

industrial park an area set aside for businesses and factories

intern a student or recent graduate who works at a job for a set period of time to get experience

pedestrian a person traveling on foot, or a word to describe something designed for walking, such as a pathway

public housing affordable rental homes provided by the government for families, senior citizens, or other people who have low incomes

suburb a smaller community outside a city, usually with many homes

urban renewal a program to replace or rebuild old or run-down buildings in a town or city

zoning the division of a large area into smaller sections or zones for specific purposes, such as residential or industrial

For More Information

Books

Lang, Glenna. *Genius of Common Sense: Jane Jacobs and the Story of The Death and Life of Great American Cities.* Boston, MA: David R. Godine, 2009.

Macaulay, David. *City: A Story of Roman Planning and Construction.* New York, NY: Houghton Mifflin, 1974.

Steele, Philip. *A City Through Time: From Ancient Colony to Vast Metropolis.* New York, NY: DK Publishing, 2013.

Websites

Next City
www.nextcity.org
Find out why and how cities are changing.

American Planning Association
www.planning.org
The American Planning Association.

Walk Score
www.walkscore.com
Get a walking score for your neighborhood.

Index